The ESSENTIALS® of
REGISTERED TRADEMARK

UNITED STATES HISTORY

— 1877 to 1912 —
Industrialism, Foreign Expansion and the Progressive Era

Salvatore Prisco III, Ph.D.
Associate Professor of Humanities
Stevens Institute of Technology
Hoboken, New Jersey

Research & Education Association
61 Ethel Road West
Piscataway, New Jersey 08854

THE ESSENTIALS ®
OF UNITED STATES HISTORY
1877 TO 1912
Industrialism, Foreign Expansion
and the Progressive Era

Printed in the United States of America

Library of Congress Catalog Card Number 97-68430

International Standard Book Number 0-87891-715-2

ESSENTIALS is a registered trademark of
Research & Education Association, Piscataway, New Jersey 08854

What the "Essentials of History" Will Do for You

REA's "Essentials of History" series offers a new approach to the study of history that is different from what has been available previously. Each book in the series has been designed to steer a sensible middle course, by including neither too much nor too little information.

Compared with conventional history outlines, the "Essentials of History" offer far more detail, with fuller explanations and interpretations of historical events and developments. Compared with voluminous historical tomes and textbooks, the "Essentials of History" offer a far more concise, less ponderous overview of each of the periods they cover.

The "Essentials of History" are intended primarily to aid students in studying history, doing homework, writing papers and preparing for exams. The books are organized to provide quick access to information and explanations of the important events, dates, and persons of the period. The books can be used in conjunction with any text. They will save hours of study and preparation time while providing a firm grasp and insightful understanding of the subject matter.

Instructors too will find the "Essentials of History" useful. The books can assist in reviewing or modifying course outlines. They also can assist with preparation of exams, as well as serve as an efficient memory refresher.

In sum, the "Essentials of History" will prove to be handy reference sources at all times.

The authors of the series are respected experts in their fields. They present clear, well-reasoned explanations and interpretations of the complex political, social, cultural, economic and philosophical issues and developments which characterize each era.

In preparing these books REA has made every effort to assure their accuracy and maximum usefulness. We are confident that each book will prove enjoyable and valuable to its user.

Dr. Max Fogiel, Program Director

About the Author

Salvatore Prisco III received his Ph.D. degree in history from Rutgers University. He has served as a tenured faculty member at the University of Alabama and the Stevens Institute of Technology in New Jersey.

Dr. Prisco is an expert in U.S. diplomatic history and foreign relations, international politics, American social and economic history, and psychohistory. He has authored books about John Barrett, a progressive era diplomat, as well as *An Introduction to Psychohistory: Theories and Case Studies.* He has published more than eighty articles, essays and book reviews.

CONTENTS

CHAPTER 1

THE NEW INDUSTRIAL ERA, 1877 – 1882

The structure of modern American society was erected by democratic, capitalistic and technological forces in the post-Civil War era. Between the 1870s and 1890s, "Gilded Age" America emerged as the world's leading industrial and agricultural producer.

1.1 POLITICS OF THE PERIOD, 1877 – 1882

The presidencies of Abraham Lincoln and Theodore Roosevelt mark the boundaries of a half century of relatively weak executive leadership, and legislative domination by Congress and the Republican Party.

1.1.1 *Disputed Election of 1876*

In 1877 the unresolved presidential election between the Republican Rutherford B. Hayes and the Democrat Samuel J.

Tilden was decided by a special electoral commission in favor of Hayes as a result of the award of 20 disputed electoral college votes from 4 states. With southern Democratic acceptance of the new Republican Hayes presidency, the last remaining Union troops were withdrawn from the Old Confederacy (South Carolina, Florida, Louisiana), and the country was at last reunified as a modern nation-state led by corporate and industrial interests. The Hayes election arrangement also marked the government's abandonment of its earlier vague commitment to African-American equality.

1.1.2 Republican Factions

"Stalwarts" led by New York Sen. Roscoe Conkling favored the old spoils system of political patronage. "Half-Breeds" headed by Maine Senator James G. Blaine pushed for civil service reform and merit appointments to government posts.

1.1.3 Election of 1880

James A. Garfield of Ohio, a Half-Breed, and his vice presidential running mate Chester A. Arthur of New York, a Stalwart, defeated the Democratic candidate, General Winfield S. Hancock of Pennsylvania and former Indiana congressman William English. Tragically the Garfield administration was but an interlude, for the President was assassinated in 1881 by a mentally disturbed patronage seeker, Charles Guiteau. Although without much executive experience, the Stalwart Arthur had the courage to endorse reform of the political spoils system by supporting passage of the Pendleton Act (1883) which established open competitive examinations for civil service positions.

1.1.4 *The Greenback-Labor Party*

This third party movement polled over 1 million votes in 1878, and elected 14 members to Congress in an effort to promote the inflation of farm prices, and the cooperative marketing of agricultural produce. In 1880, the party's presidential candidate, James Weaver of Iowa, advocated public control and regulation of private enterprises such as railroads in the common interest of more equitable competition. Weaver theorized that because railroads were so essential, they should be treated as a public utility. He polled only 3 percent of the vote.

1.2 THE ECONOMY, 1877 – 1882

Industrial expansion and technology assumed major proportions in this period. Between 1860 and 1894 the United States moved from the fourth largest manufacturing nation to the world's leader through capital accumulation, natural resources, especially in iron, oil, and coal, an abundance of labor helped by massive immigration, railway transportation and communications (the telephone was introduced by Alexander Graham Bell in 1876), and major technical innovations such as the development of the modern steel industry by Andrew Carnegie, and electrical energy by Thomas Edison. In the petroleum industry, John D. Rockefeller controlled 95 percent of the U.S. oil refineries by 1877.

1.2.1 *The New South*

By 1880, northern capital erected the modern textile industry in the New South by bringing factories to the cotton fields. Birmingham, Alabama emerged as the South's leading steel producer, and the introduction of machine-made cigarettes propelled the Duke family to prominence as tobacco producers.

3

1.2.2 Standard of Living

Throughout the U.S. the standard of living rose sharply, but the distribution of wealth was very uneven. Increasingly an elite of about 10 per cent of the population controlled 90 per cent of the nation's wealth.

1.2.3 Social Darwinism

Many industrial leaders used the doctrines associated with the "Gospel of Wealth" to justify the unequal distribution of national wealth. Self-justification by the wealthy was based on the notion that God had granted wealth as He had given grace for material and spiritual salvation of the select few. These few, according to William Graham Sumner, relied heavily on the survival-of-the-fittest philosophy associated with Charles Darwin.

1.2.4 Labor Unrest

When capital over-expansion and over-speculation led to the economic panic of 1873, massive labor disorders spread through the country leading to the paralyzing railroad strike of 1877. Unemployment and salary reductions caused major class conflict. President Hayes used federal troops to restore order after dozens of workers were killed. Immigrant workers began fighting among themselves in California where Irish and Chinese laborers fought for economic survival.

1.2.5 Labor Unions

The depression of the 1870s undermined national labor organizations. The National Labor Union (1866) had a membership of 600,000 but failed to withstand the impact of economic adversity. The Knights of Labor (1869) managed to open its

GROWTH OF INDUSTRY AND CITIES, 1900

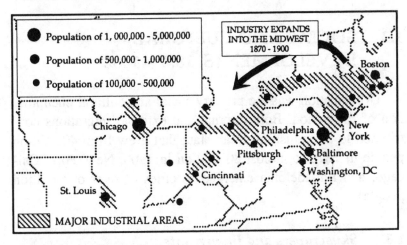

membership to not only white native American workers, but immigrants, women and African-Americans as well. Although they claimed one million members, they too could not weather the hard times of the 1870s, and eventually went under in 1886 in the wake of the bloody Haymarket Riot in Chicago.

1.2.6 *Agricultural Militancy*

Agrarian discontent expressed through the activities of the National Grange and the Farmers' Alliances in the West and South showed greater lasting power. During the Civil War, many farmers had over-expanded their operations, purchased more land and machinery, and went heavily into debt. When the relatively high wartime agricultural prices collapsed in the decades after the war, farmers worked collectively to promote currency inflation, higher farm prices, silver and gold bimetalism, debt relief, cooperative farm marketing ventures, and regulation of monopolies and railroads by the federal and state governments. Although not very successful in the 1870s, farmer militancy continued to be a powerful political and economic force in the decades of the 1880s and 1890s.

1.3   SOCIAL AND CULTURAL DEVELOPMENTS, 1877 – 1882

Urbanization was the primary social and cultural phenomenon of the period. Both internal and external migrations contributed to an industrial urban state that grew from 40 million people in 1870 to almost 80 million in 1900. New York, Chicago, and Philadelphia emerged as cities of over one million people.

1.3.1   *Skyscrapers and Immigrants*

Cities grew both up and out as the skyscraper made its appearance after the introduction of the mechanical elevator by Elisha Otis. The city also grew outward into a large, impersonal metropolis divided into various business, industrial and residential sectors, usually segregated by ethnic group, social class and race. Slums and tenements sprang up within walking distance of department stores and town houses. Two million immigrants from northern Europe poured into the U.S. during the 1870s. In the 1880s another five million entered the country, but by this time they were coming from southern and eastern Europe. Many people faced the dual difficulty of migration from one culture to another, and also migration from a predominantly rural lifestyle to an urban one in the United States.

1.3.2   *Lack of Government Policy*

There were few programs to deal with the vast influx of humanity other than the prohibition of the criminal and the insane. City governments soon developed the primary responsibility for immigrants – often trading employment, housing and social services for political support.

1.3.3 Social Gospel

In time, advocates of the "social gospel" such as Jane Addams and Washington Gladden urged the creation of settlement houses and better health and education services to accommodate the new immigrants. New religions also appeared including the Salvation Army, and Mary Baker Eddy's Church of Christian Science in 1879.

1.3.4 Education

Public education continued to expand, especially on the secondary level. Private Catholic parochial schools and teaching colleges grew in number as well. Adult education and English instruction became important functions of both public and private schooling.

1.3.5 African-American Leaders

Booker T. Washington emerged in 1881 as the president of Tuskegee Institute in Alabama, a school devoted to teaching and vocational education for African-Americans with a mission to encourage self-respect and economic equality of the races. It was at Tuskegee that George Washington Carver emerged in subsequent years as an agricultural chemist who did much to find industrial applications for agricultural products.

1.3.6 Feminism

The new urban environment encouraged feminist activism.

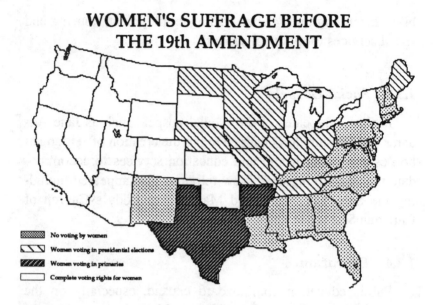

WOMEN'S SUFFRAGE BEFORE THE 19th AMENDMENT

No voting by women
Women voting in presidential elections
Women voting in primaries
Complete voting rights for women

Millions of women worked outside the home, and continued to demand voting rights. Many women became active in social reform movements such as the prohibitionist Women's Christian Temperance Movement, planned parenthood, humane societies, anti-prostitution crusades, and equal rights for all regardless of gender, race, and class.

1.3.7 Literature

Important books appeared such as Henry George's *Progress and Poverty*, 1879, a 3 million copy seller that advocated one single tax on land as the means to redistribute wealth for greater social and economic justice. In fiction Lew Wallace's *Ben Hur*, 1880, and the many Horatio Alger stories promoting values such as hard work, honesty, and a touch of good fortune sold many millions of copies. Other famous works of the era included Mark Twain's *The Gilded Age*, 1873, and *The Adventures of Tom Sawyer*, 1876, Bret Harte's stories of the old

West, William Dean Howell's social commentaries, Henry James' *Daisy Miller*, 1879, and *The Portrait of the Lady*, 1881.

1.4 FOREIGN RELATIONS, 1877 – 1882

The United States gradually became involved in the "new imperialism" of the 1870s geared to finding markets for surplus industrial production, access to needed raw materials, and opportunities for overseas investment during a time of domestic economic depression. Unlike European territorial colonialism, however, the United States preferred market expansion without the political liability of military occupation.

1.4.1 *Latin America*

President Hayes recognized the government of dictator Porfirio Diaz in Mexico thus encouraging not only trade expansion, but U.S. investment in railroads, mines, agriculture and oil.

1.4.2 *Pan Americanism*

In 1881 Secretary of State James G. Blaine advocated the creation of an International Bureau of American Republics to promote a customs union of trade and political stability for the western hemisphere. The assassination of President Garfield temporarily kept Blaine from forming this organization until 1889. The Bureau subsequently evolved into the Pan American Union in 1910, and the Organization of American States in 1948.

1.4.3 *Mediation of Border Disputes*

The United States offered its good offices to promote the

peaceful resolution of border conflicts between a number of states: in 1876 between Argentina and Paraguay; in 1880 between Colombia and Chile; in 1881 between Mexico and Guatemala, Argentina and Chile, and Peru and Chile. The United States also worked to bring an end to the War of the Pacific (1879 – 1884) fought between Chile and the alliance of Peru and Bolivia.

1.4.4 Canal Project

In 1876 the Interoceanic Canal Commission recommended a Nicaraguan route for a canal to link the Atlantic and Pacific Oceans. In the 1880s, the U.S. officially took a hostile position against the French Panama Canal project.

1.4.5 The Pacific

In 1878, the United States ratified a treaty with Samoa giving the U.S. trading rights and a naval base at Pago Pago.

1.4.6 Japan

In 1878, the United States was the first country to negotiate a treaty granting tariff autonomy to Japan, and set a precedent for ending the practice by western nations of controlling customs house collections in Asian states.

1.4.7 Korea

Commodore Shufeldt opened trade and diplomatic relations with the Hermit Kingdom in 1882. The United States promoted the principles of equal opportunity of trade, and the sovereignty of Korea (later known as open door policies) which had earlier been advocated as desirable in China.

1.4.8 Native Americans

Westward expansion and the discovery of gold in South Dakota in the early 1870s led to the Sioux War, 1876 – 1877, and George A. Custer's "last stand." In 1877 the Nez Perce War in Idaho resulted from similar causes. The Apache in Arizona and New Mexico fought as well.

1.4.9 Reservations

The Indian tribes were eventually vanquished and compelled to live on isolated reservations. In addition to superior U.S. military force, disease, railway construction, alcoholism, and the virtual extermination of the bison contributed to their defeat. In 1881 Helen Hunt Jackson's *A Century of Dishonor* chronicled the tragic policy pursued against the Native Americans.

CHAPTER 2

THE REACTION TO CORPORATE INDUSTRIALISM, 1882 – 1887

The rise of big business and monopoly capitalism – especially in banking, railroads, mining, and the oil and steel industries – generated a reaction on the part of working class Americans in the form of new labor organizations and collective political action. Most Americans, however, were not opposed to free enterprise economics, but simply wanted an opportunity to share in the profits.

2.1   POLITICS OF THE PERIOD, 1882 – 1887

The only Democrat elected President in the half century after the Civil War was Grover Cleveland.

2.1.1 *Election of 1884*

The Republicans nominated James G. Blaine (Maine) for president and John Logan (Illinois) for vice-president. The Democrats chose New York governor Grover Cleveland and Thomas A. Hendricks (Indiana). The defection of Independent Republicans supporting civil service reforms, known as "Mugwumps" (such as E.L. Godkin and Carl Schurz) to the Cleveland camp cost Blaine, the former Speaker of the House, the election. The Democrats held control of the House and the Republicans controlled the Senate.

2.1.2 *Presidential Succession Act of 1886*

The death of Vice-President Hendricks in 1885 led to a decision to change the line of succession (established in 1792) from the president pro tempore of the Senate to the Cabinet officers in order of creation of their departments to maintain party leadership. This system lasted until 1947 when the Speaker of the House was declared third in line.

2.1.3 *Executive Appointments*

President Cleveland insisted that executive appointments and removals were the prerogative of the executive and not the Senate. This was the first time since Andrew Johnson that a president had strengthened the independence of his office.

2.2 THE ECONOMY, 1882 – 1887

Large, efficient corporations prospered. Captains of industry, or robber barons, such as John D. Rockefeller in oil, J.P. Morgan in banking, Gustavus Swift in meat processing, Andrew Carnegie in steel, and E. H. Harriman in railroads, put together major industrial empires.

2.2.1 *Big Business*

The concentration of wealth and power in the hands of a relatively small number of giant firms in many industries led to monopoly capitalism that minimized competition. This process, in turn, led to a demand by smaller businessmen, farmers and laborers for government regulation of the economy in order to promote capital competition for the salvation of free enterprise economics.

2.2.2 *The Interstate Commerce Act* (1887)

Popular resentment of railroad abuses such as price fixing, kickbacks, and discriminatory freight rates created demands for state regulation of the railway industry. When the Supreme Court ruled individual state laws unconstitutional (Wabash Case, 1886) because only Congress had the right to control interstate commerce, the Interstate Commerce Act was passed providing that a commission be established to oversee fair and just railway rates, prohibit rebates, end discriminatory practices, and require annual reports and financial statements. The Supreme Court, however, remained a friend of special interests, and often undermined the work of the I.C.C.

2.2.3 *Expanding Cultivation*

Agrarians and ranchers continued their westward expansion. The amount of land under cultivation between 1870 and 1890 more than doubled from 408 to 840 million acres. Transcontinental railroads, modern farm machinery, and soil conservation practices contributed to national prosperity.

2.2.4 *Low Farm Prices*

Despite success, many farmers were concerned about capital indebtedness, low farm prices resulting from surplus production, railroad rate discrimination, and the lack of sufficient silver currency to promote price inflation. Agrarian groups such as the National Grange and the Farmers' Alliances called for government regulation of the economy to redress their grievances. To a certain extent, however, many of these problems were determined by participation of American agriculture in global markets. Farmers did not completely understand all the risks in an international free market economy.

2.2.5 *American Federation of Labor, 1886*

Confronted by big business, Samuel Gompers and Adolph Strasser put together a combination of national craft unions to represent the material interests of labor in the matter of wages, hours, and safety conditions. The A.F. of L. philosophy was pragmatic and not directly influenced by the dogmatic Marxism of some European labor movements. Although militant in its use of the strike, and its demand for collective bargaining in labor contracts with large corporations such as those in railroads, mining and manufacturing, the A.F. of L. did not intend violent revolution or political radicalism.

2.2.6 *Scientific Management*

Frederick W. Taylor, the father of scientific management, introduced modern concepts of industrial engineering, plant management, time and motion studies, and a separate class of managers in industrial manufacturing.

2.2.7   Tariff Policy

Although still protecting many American industries, the tariff of 1883 lowered duty schedules by an average 5 percent.

2.3   SOCIAL AND CULTURAL DEVELOPMENTS, 1882 – 1887

The continued growth of urban America contributed to the dissemination of knowledge and information in many fields.

2.3.1   Newspapers and Magazines

The linotype machine (1886) invented by Otto Mergenthaler cut printing costs dramatically. Press associations flourished and publishing became big business. In 1884, Joseph Pulitzer, a Hungarian-born immigrant, was the first publisher to reach a mass audience when he sold 100,000 copies of the New York *World*. New magazines such as *Forum* appeared in 1886, and they often featured a hard-hitting editorial style that emphasized investigatory journalism and controversial subjects.

2.3.2   Higher Education

Colleges and universities expanded and introduced a more modern curriculum. Graduate study emphasized meticulous research and the seminar method as pioneered in the United States at Johns Hopkins University. A complex society required a more professional and specialized education.

2.3.3   Women's Colleges

Bryn Mawr (1885) was established and soon found a place

among such schools as Vassar, Wellesley, and Mount Holyoke in advancing education for women.

2.3.4 *Natural Science*

Albert Michelson at the University of Chicago, working on the speed of light, contributed in the 1880s to theories which helped prepare the way for Einstein's theory of relativity. In 1907, Michelson was the first American to win a Nobel Prize.

2.3.5 *The New Social Science*

Richard T. Ely studied the ethical implications of economic problems. Henry C. Adams and Simon Patten put forth theories to justify government regulation and planning in the economy. In sociology, Lester Frank Ward's *Dynamic Sociology* (1883) stressed intelligent planning and decision making over genetic determinism as promoted by Social Darwinists such as William Graham Sumner. Woodrow Wilson's *Congressional Government* was a critique of the committee system in Congress and called for a better working relationship between the executive and legislative branches of government. After winning the presidency in 1912, Wilson would be in a position to put his ideas into practice.

2.3.6 *Literary Realism*

Romanticism declined in favor of a more realistic approach to literature. Novelists explored social problems such as crime and political corruption, urban ghetto life, class conflict, evolution and the environment. Mark Twain's masterpiece *Huckleberry Finn* appeared in 1884. In 1885, William Dean Howell's *The Rise of Silas Lapham* presented the theme of business ethics in a competitive society. *The Bostonians* (1886) by Henry

James attempted a complex psychological study of female behavior.

2.3.7 *Art*

Realism could also be seen in the artistic works of Thomas Eakins, Mary Cassatt, Winslow Homer, and James Whistler. Museums and art schools expanded. Wealthy patrons spent fortunes on personal art collections. Immigrant artists attracted enthusiastic crowds to settlement house exhibits.

2.4   FOREIGN RELATIONS, 1882 – 1887

Contrary to popular belief, the United States was not an isolationist nation in the 1880s. Trade expansion and the protection of markets were primary concerns.

2.4.1 *Modern Navy*

In 1883 Congress authorized the construction of new steel ships that would take the U.S. Navy in a 20-year period from twelfth to third in world naval ranking. In 1884, the U.S. Naval War College was established in Newport, Rhode Island, the first of its kind.

2.4.2 *Europe*

Problems existed with Britain over violence in Ireland and England. In 1886, the U.S. refused to extradite an Irish national accused of terrorist activity in London.

Diseased meat products in the European market led to British and German bans against uninspected American meat exports. Congress soon provided for government regulation and inspection of meat for export. This action would set a precedent for systematic food and drug inspection in later years.

2.4.3 *Africa*

The United States participated in the Berlin Conference (1884) concerning trade in the Congo. The U.S. also took part in the Third International Red Cross Conference.

2.4.4 *Asia*

In 1882, Congress passed a law suspending Chinese immigration to the U.S. for ten years. The act reflected racist American attitudes and created friction with China.

2.4.5 *The Pacific*

In 1886, the U.S. obtained by treaty with Hawaii the Pearl Harbor Naval Base.

2.4.6 *Missionaries*

American Christian missionaries were active in the Pacific, Asia, Africa, Latin America and the Middle East. Missionaries not only brought religion to many third world regions, but also western education, exposure to science and technology, and commercial ventures. Some missionaries also took with them racist concepts of white supremacy.

2.4.7 *Latin America*

In 1884, the U.S. signed a short-lived pact with Nicaragua for joint ownership of an Isthmian canal in Central America.

CHAPTER 3

THE EMERGENCE OF REGIONAL EMPIRE, 1887 – 1892

Despite a protective tariff policy, the United States became increasingly international as it sought to export surplus manufactured and agricultural goods. Foreign markets were viewed as a safety valve for labor employment problems and agrarian unrest. The return of Secretary of State James G. Blaine in 1889 marked a major attempt by the United States to promote a regional empire in the western hemisphere and reciprocal trade programs.

3.1   POLITICS OF THE PERIOD, 1887 – 1892

National politics became more controversial and turbulent in this era.

3.1.1 Election of 1888

Although the Democrat Grover Cleveland won the popular vote by about 100,000 over the Republican Benjamin Harrison, Harrison carried the electoral college 233 – 168, and was declared president after waging a vigorous campaign to protect American industrial interests with a high protective tariff. In Congress, Republicans won control of both the House and Senate.

3.1.2 Department of Agriculture

The Department of Agriculture (1889) was raised to Cabinet status with Norman Coleman as the first secretary.

3.1.3 House Rules of Operation

Republican Thomas B. Reed became Speaker of the House in 1890, and changed the rules of operation to make himself a veritable tsar with absolute control in running the House.

3.1.4 Force Bill (1890)

Senate objections kept Congress from protecting African-American voters in the South through federal supervision of state elections.

3.1.5 Dependent Pensions Act (1890)

Congress granted service pensions to Union veterans and their dependents for the first time.

3.2   THE ECONOMY, 1887 – 1892

Anti-monopoly measures, protective tariffs and reciprocal trade, and a billion dollar budget became the order of the day.

3.2.1   *Sherman Anti-Trust Act* (1890)

Corporate monopolies (trusts) which controlled whole industries were subject to federal prosecution if they were found to be combinations or conspiracies in restraint of trade. Although supported by smaller businesses, labor unions and farm associations, the Sherman Anti-Trust Act was in time interpreted by the Supreme Court to apply to labor unions and farmers' cooperatives as much as to large corporate combinations. Monopoly was still dominant over laissez-faire, free enterprise economics during the decade of the 1890s.

3.2.2   *Sherman Silver Purchase Act* (1890)

Pro-silver interests passed legislation authorizing Congress to buy 4.5 million ounces of silver each month at market prices, and issue Treasury notes redeemable in gold and silver. The Act created inflation and lowered gold reserves.

3.2.3   *McKinley Tariff* (1890)

This compromise protective tariff promised by the Republicans in 1888, and introduced by William McKinley of Ohio was passed and extended to industrial and agricultural goods. The Act also included reciprocal trade provisions that allowed the president to retaliate against nations that discriminated against U.S. products, and reward states that opened their markets to American goods. Subsequent price increases led to a popular backlash, and a Democratic House victory in the 1890 congressional elections.

3.2.4 *Billion Dollar Budget*

Congress depleted the Treasury surplus with the first peacetime billion dollar appropriation of funds for state tax refunds, infrastructure improvements, navy modernization, and pension payments. The loss of Treasury reserves put the economy in a precarious position when an economic panic occurred in 1893.

3.3 SOCIAL AND CULTURAL DEVELOPMENTS, 1887 – 1892

Amusing the millions became a popular pastime.

3.3.1 *Popular Amusements*

In addition to the legitimate stage, vaudeville shows presenting variety acts became immensely popular. The circus expanded when Barnum and Bailey formed a partnership to present "the greatest show on earth." Distinctively American Wild West shows toured North America and Europe. To record these activities, George Eastman's newly invented roll-film camera became popular with spectators.

3.3.2 *Sports*

In 1888, professional baseball sent an all-star team to tour the world. Boxing adopted leather golves in 1892. Croquet and bicycle racing were new crazes. Basketball was invented in 1891 by James Naismith, a Massachusetts Y.M.C.A. instructor. Organized inter-collegiate sports such as football, basketball and baseball created intense rivalries between colleges that attracted mass spectator interest.

3.3.3   *Childrearing Practices*

Parents became more supportive and sympathetic to their children and less authoritarian and restrictive. The 1880s were something of a golden age in children's literature. Mary Wells Smith depicted an agrarian ideal; Sidney Lanier wrote tales of heroic boys and girls; Howard Pyle's Robin Hood gained wide readership and Joel Chandler Harris' characters Brer Rabbit, Brer Fox and Uncle Remus became very popular.

3.3.4   *Religion*

Many churches took issue with the growing emphasis on materialism in American society. Dwight Lyman Moody introduced Urban revivalism comparable to earlier rural movements among Protestant denominations. In addition, the new immigrants generated significant growth for Roman Catholicism and Judaism. By 1890, there about 150 religious denominations in the United States.

3.4   FOREIGN RELATIONS, 1887 – 1892

Following in the footsteps of William Seward as a major architect of American foreign policy, James G. Blaine promoted hemispheric solidarity with Latin America and economic expansionism.

3.4.1   *Pan Americanism*

As Secretary of State, Blaine was concerned with international trade, political stability and excessive militarism in Latin

24

America. His international Bureau of American Republics was designed to promote a Pan American customs union and peaceful conflict resolution. To achieve his aims, Blaine opposed U.S. military intervention in the hemisphere. To a certain extent, his policies were in the tradition of President James Monroe and his Secretary of State, John Quincy Adams.

3.4.2 Haiti

After the Haitian revolution of 1888 – 1889, Blaine resisted pressure for U.S. intervention to establish a naval base near Port-au-Prince. The noted African-American Frederick Douglas played a key role in advising Blaine as U.S. minister to Haiti.

3.4.3 Chilean Revolution

When American sailors from the U.S.S. *Baltimore* were killed in Valparaiso (1891), President Harrison threatened war with the anti-American revolutionary government of President Balmaceda. Secretary Blaine helped to bring about a Chilean apology and preserve his Pan American policy.

3.4.4 Asia and the Pacific

Korea. The medical missionary/diplomat, Horace Allen promoted peaceful American investment and trade with Korea.

Samoa. In 1889, the United States upheld its interests against German expansion in the Samoan Islands by establishing a 3-party protectorate over Samoa with Britain and Germany. The United States retained the port of Pago Pago.

Hawaii. In 1891, Queen Liliuokalani resisted American attempts to promote a protectorate over Hawaii. By 1893, pro-American sugar planters overthrew the native Hawaiian government and established a new government friendly to the United States.

3.4.5 Africa

The United States refused (1890) naval bases in the Portuguese colonies of Angola and Mozambique when Portugal was looking for allies against British expansion in Africa. Blaine opposed territorial expansion for the U.S. in Africa, but favored the development of commercial markets.

3.4.6 Theoretical Works

In 1890, Naval Captain Alfred Thayer Mahan published *The Influence of Sea Power on History* which argued that control of the seas was the means to world power. Josiah Strong's *Our Country* presented the thesis that Americans had a mission to fulfill by exporting the word of God around the world, especially to non-white populations. Frederick Jackson Turner's "Frontier Thesis" (1893) justified overseas economic expansion as a way to secure political power and prosperity. In *The Law of Civilization and Decay* (1895), Brooks Adams postulated that a nation must expand or face inevitable decline.

3.4.7 Europe

The murders of eleven Italian citizens in New Orleans (1891) brought the United States and Italy into confrontation. The United States defused the situation by compensating the families of the victims.

CHAPTER 4

ECONOMIC DEPRESSION AND SOCIAL CRISIS, 1892 – 1897

The economic depression that began in 1893 brought about a collective response from organized labor, militant agriculture and the business community. Each group called for economic safeguards, and a more humane free enterprise system that would expand economic opportunities in an equitable manner.

4.1 POLITICS OF THE PERIOD, 1892 – 1897

The most marked development in American politics was the emergence of a viable third party movement in the form of the essentially agrarian Populist Party.

4.1.1 *Election of 1892*

Democrat Grover Cleveland (NY) and his vice presidential running mate Adlai E. Stevenson (IL) regained the White House by defeating the Republican President Benjamin Harrison (IN) and Vice President Whitelaw Reid (NY). Voters generally reacted against the inflationary McKinley Tariff. Cleveland's conservative economic stand in favor of the gold standard brought him the support of various business interests. The Democrats won control of both houses of Congress.

4.1.2 *Populist Party*

The People's Party (Populist) nominated James Weaver (Iowa) for president and James Field (Virginia) for vice president in 1892. The party platform put together by such Populist leaders as Ignatius Donnally (Minnesota), Thomas Watson (Georgia), Mary Lease (Kansas), and "Sockless" Jerry Simpson (Kansas) called for the enactment of a program espoused by agrarians, but also for a coalition with urban workers and the middle class. Specific goals were the coinage of silver to gold at a ratio of 16 to 1; federal loans to farmers; a graduated income tax; postal savings banks; public ownership of railroads, telephone and telegraph systems; prohibition of alien land ownership; immigration restriction; a ban on private armies used by corporations to break up strikes; an 8-hour working day; a single six-year term for president, and direct election of senators; the right of initiative and referendum; and the use of the secret ballot.

Although the Populists were considered radical by some, they actually wanted to reform the system from within, and allow for a fairer distribution of wealth. In a society in which 10 percent of the population controlled 90 percent of the nation's wealth, the Populists were able to garner about one million votes (out of 11 million votes cast), and 22 electoral votes. By 1894, Populists had elected 4 senators, 4 congressmen, 21 state executive officials, 150 state senators, and 315 state representatives, primarily in the West and South. After the 1893 depression, the Populists planned a serious bid for national power in the 1896 election.

4.1.3 *Repeal of Sherman Silver Purchase Act* (1893)

After the economic panic of 1893, Cleveland tried to limit the outflow of gold reserves by asking Congress to repeal the Sherman Silver Act which had provided for notes redemptive in either gold or silver. Congress did repeal the act, but the Democratic Party split over the issue.

4.1.4 *Election of 1896*

The Republicans nominated William McKinley (Ohio) for president and Garrett Hobart (New Jersey) for vice president on a platform calling for maintaining the gold standard and protective tariffs. The Democratic Party repudiated Cleveland's conservative economics and nominated William Jennings Bryan (Nebraska) and Arthur Sewell (Maine) for president and vice president on a platform similar to the Populists: 1) coinage of silver at a ratio of 16 to 1; 2) condemnation of monopolies, protective tariffs and anti-union court injunctions; 3) criticism of the Supreme Court's removal of a graduated income tax from the Wilson-Gorman tariff bill (1894). Bryan delivered one of the most famous speeches in American history when he declared that the people must not be "crucified upon a cross of gold."

The Populist Party also nominated Bryan, but chose

Thomas Watson (Georgia) for vice president. Having been out-maneuvered by the Silver Democrats, the Populists lost the opportunity to become a permanent political force.

McKinley won a hard fought election by only about one-half million votes as Republicans succeeded in creating fear among business groups and middle class voters that Bryan represented a revolutionary challenge to the American system. The manipulation of higher farm prices, and the warning to labor unions that they would face unemployment if Bryan won the election helped to tilt the vote in favor of McKinley. An often forgotten issue in 1896 was the Republican promise to stabilize the ongoing Cuban revolution. This pledge would eventually lead the U.S. into war with Spain (1898) for Cuban independence. The Republicans retained control over Congress which they had gained in 1894.

4.2   THE ECONOMY, 1892 – 1897

The 1890s was a period of economic depression and labor agitation.

4.2.1   *Homestead Strike* (1892)

Iron and steel workers went on strike in Pennsylvania against the Carnegie Steel Co. to protest salary reductions. Carnegie employed strike-breaking Pinkerton security guards. Management-labor warfare led to a number of deaths on both sides.

4.2.2   *Depression of 1893*

The primary causes for the Depression of 1893 were the dramatic growth of federal deficit; withdrawal of British investments from the American market and the outward transfer of gold; loss of business confidence; and the bankruptcy of the National Cordage Co. was the first among thousands of U.S. corporations that closed banks and businesses. As a consequence, 20 percent of the work force was eventually unemployed. The depression would last four years. Recovery would be helped by war preparation.

4.2.3 March of Unemployed (1894)

The Populist businessman Jocob Coxey led a march of hundreds of unemployed workers on Washington asking for a government work relief program. The government met the marchers with force and arrested their leaders.

4.2.4 Pullman Strike (1894)

Eugene Debs' American Railway Union struck the Pullman Palace Car Co. in Chicago over wage cuts and job losses. President Cleveland broke the violent strike with federal troops. Popular opinion deplored violence and militant labor tactics.

4.2.5 Wilson-Gorman Tariff (1894)

This protective tariff did little to promote overseas trade as a way to ease the depression. A provision amended to create a graduated income tax was stricken by the Supreme Court as unconstitutional (*Pollack v. Farmers' Loan and Trust Co.*, 1895).

4.2.6 Dingley Tariff (1897)

The Dingley Tariff raised protection to new highs for certain commodities.

4.2.7 *Surplus Production and Foreign Trade*

Anxiety over domestic class warfare, and the desire to sell surplus manufactured goods overseas led many business interests to encourage the U.S. government to find new international markets. Carnegie Steel and Standard Oil lobbied the State Department for better trade promotion policies as a way to recover from the depression, and provide jobs for American workers. Ironically, special business interests often undercut efforts to establish reciprocal trade agreements and free trade in favor of politically motivated tariff protection.

4.3 SOCIAL AND CULTURAL DEVELOPMENTS, 1892 – 1897

Economic depression and war dominated thought and literature in the decade of the 1890s.

4.3.1 *Literature*

Lester Frank Ward of Brown University presented a critique of excessive competition in favor of social planning in *The Psychic Factors of Civilization* (1893). William Dean Howells' *A Hazard of New Fortunes* (1890), was a broad attack on urban living conditions in industrial America, and the callous treatment of workers by wealthy tycoons. Stephen Crane wrote about the abuse of control of women in *Maggie, A Girl of the Streets* (1892), and the pain of war in *The Red Badge of Courage* (1895). Edward Bellamy's *Looking Backward* presented a science fiction look into a prosperous, but regimented future.

Americans also began to read such European realists as

Dostoevsky, Ibsen, Tolstoy and Zola.

William James' *Principles of Psychology* introduced the discipline to American readers as a modern science of the human mind.

4.3.2 *Prohibition of Alcohol*

The Anti-Saloon League was formed in 1893. Women were especially concerned about the increase of drunkenness during the depression.

4.3.3 *Immigration*

Immigration declined by almost 400,000 during the depression. Jane Addams' Hull House in Chicago continued to function as a means of settling poor immigrants from Greece, Germany, Italy, Poland, Russia and elsewhere into American society. Lillian Wald's Henry Street Settlement in New York, and Robert Wood's South End House in Boston performed similar functions. Such institutions also lobbied against sweatshop labor conditions, and for bans on child labor.

4.3.4 *Chautaugua Movement*

Home study courses growing out of the Chautaugua Movement in New York State became popular.

4.3.5 *Chicago World's Fair* (1893)

Beautifying the cities was the Fair's main theme. One lasting development was the expansion of urban public parks.

4.3.6 *Radio and Film*

Nathan Stubblefield transmitted voice over the air without wires in 1892. Thomas Edison's kinetoscope permitted the viewing of motion pictures in 1893.

4.4 FOREIGN RELATIONS, 1892 – 1897

In addition to the economic depression, three international events in 1895 that propelled the United States foreign policy were the Cuban war for independence against Spain, Britain's boundary dispute with Venezuela and the settlement of the Sino-Japanese War.

4.4.1 *Cuba and Spain*

The Cuban revolt against Spain in 1895 impacted on the U.S. in that Americans had about $50 million invested in the Cuban economy, and did an annual business of over $100 million in Cuba. During the election of 1896, McKinley promised to stabilize the situation and work for an end to hostilities. Sensational "yellow" journalism, and nationalistic statements from officials such as Assistant Secretary of the Navy, Theodore Roosevelt, encouraged popular support for direct American military intervention on behalf of Cuban independence. President McKinley, however, proceeded cautiously through 1897.

4.4.2 *Britain and Venezuela* (1895)

The dispute over the border of Britain's colony of Guiana threatened war with Venezuela, especially after gold was discovered in the area. Although initially at odds with Britain, the

United States eventually came to support British claims against Venezuela when Britain agreed to recognize the Monroe Doctrine in Latin America. Britain also sought U.S. cooperation in its dispute with Germany in South Africa. This rivalry would in time lead to the Boer War. The realignment of the United States and Britain would play a significant role during World War I.

4.4.3　*The Sino-Japanese War* (1894 – 1895)

Japan's easy victory over China signaled to the United States and other nations trading in Asia that China's weakness might result in its colonization by industrial powers, and the closing of the China market. The U.S. resolved to seek a naval base in the Pacific to protect its interests. The opportunity to annex the Philippines after the war with Spain was in part motivated by the desire to protect America's trade and future potential in Asia. This concern would also lead the U.S. to announce the Open Door policy with China in 1899 and 1900 designed to protect equal opportunity of trade, and China's political independence.

4.4.4　*Latin America*

When revolutions broke out in 1894 in both Brazil and Nicaragua, the United States supported the existing governments in power to maintain political stability and favorable trade treaties. Secretaries of State Walter Q. Gresham, Richard Olney and John Sherman continued to support James G. Blaine's Pan American policy.

4.4.5 *The Pacific*

The United States intervened in the Hawaiian revolution (1893) to overthrow the anti-American government of Queen Liliuokalani. President Cleveland rejected American annexation of Hawaii in 1894, but President McKinley agreed to annex it in 1898.

CHAPTER 5

WAR AND THE AMERICANIZATION OF THE WORLD, 1897 – 1902

In 1900, an Englishman named William T. Stead authored a book entitled *The Americanization of the World* in which he predicted that American productivity and economic strength would propel the United States to the forefront of world leadership in the 20th century. The Spanish-American War and the events following it indicated that the U.S. would be a force in the global balance of power for years to come. Few, however, would have predicted that as early as 1920 the U.S. would achieve the pinnacle of world power as a result of the debilitating policies pursued by European political leaders during World War I (1914 – 1919). One question remained: Would the American people be prepared to accept the responsibility of world leadership?

5.1 POLITICS OF THE PERIOD, 1897 – 1902

President McKinley's wartime leadership and tragic assassination closed one door in American history, but opened another door to the leadership of Theodore Roosevelt, the first "progressive" president.

5.1.1 *Election of 1900*

The unexpected death of Vice President Garrett Hobart led the Republican Party to choose the war hero and reform governor of New York, Theodore Roosevelt, as President William McKinley's vice presidential running mate. Riding the crest of victory against Spain, the G.O.P platform called for upholding the gold standard for full economic recovery, promoting economic expansion and power in the Caribbean and the Pacific, and building a canal in Central America. The Democrats nominated once again William Jennings Bryan and Adlai Stevenson on a platform condemning imperialism and the gold standard. McKinley easily won reelection by about 1 million votes (7.2 million to 6.3 million), and the Republicans retained control of both houses of Congress.

5.1.2 *Other Parties*

The fading Populists nominated Wharton Barker (Pennsylvania) and Ignatius Donnelly (Minnesota) on a pro-inflation platform but only received 50,000 votes. The Socialist Democratic Party nominated Eugene V. Debs (Indiana) and Job Harriman (California)·on a platform urging the nationalization of major industries. Debs received 94,000 votes. The surprising Prohibition Party nominated John Woolley (Illinois) and Henry Metcalf (Rhode Island) and called for a ban on alcohol production and consumption. They received 209,000 votes.

5.1.3 *McKinley Assassination* (1901)

While attending the Pan American Exposition in Buffalo, New York, the President was shot on Sept. 6 by Leon Czolgosz, an anarchist sworn to destroy all governments. The President died on Sept. 14 after many officials thought he would recover. Theodore Roosevelt became the nation's 25th president and its youngest to that time at age 42.

5.2 THE ECONOMY, 1897 – 1902

The war with Spain provided the impetus for economic recovery. President Roosevelt promised a "square deal" for all Americans, farmers, workers, consumers and businessmen. Progressive economic reform was geared to the rejuvination of free enterprise capitalism following the 1893 depression, and the destruction of illegal monopolies. In this way, radicals would be denied an audience for more revolutionary and violent change.

5.2.1 *War With Spain* (1898)

The financial cost of the war was $250,000,000. Eastern and mid-western industrial cities tended to favor war and benefit from it. Northeastern financial centers were more cautious about war until March 1898, and questioned the financial gains of wartime production at the expense of peacetime expansion and product/market development.

5.2.2 *Federal Bankruptcy Act* (1898)

This act reformed and standardized procedures for bankruptcy, and the responsibilities of creditors and debtors.

5.2.3 *Erdman Act* (1898)

This act provided for mediation by the chair of the Interstate Commerce Commission and the commissioner of the Bureau of Labor in unresolved railroad labor controversies.

5.2.4 *Currency Act* (1900)

The United States standardized the amount of gold in the dollar at 25.8 grains, 9/10s fine. A separate gold reserve was set apart from other general funds, and government bonds were sold to maintain the reserve.

5.2.5 *Technology*

Between 1860 and 1900 railroad trackage grew from 36,800 miles to 193,350 miles. U.S. Steel Corp. was formed in 1901, Standard Oil Company of New Jersey in 1899.

5.3 SOCIAL AND CULTURAL DEVELOPMENTS, 1897 - 1902

Debates about the war and territorial acquisitions, and the state of the economy, tended to dominate thought and literature.

5.3.1 *Yellow Journalism*

Joseph Pulitzer's New York *World* and William Randolph Hearst's New York *Journal* competed fiercely to increase circulation through exaggeration of Spanish atrocities in Cuba. Such stories whipped up popular resentment of Spain, and helped to create a climate of opinion receptive to war.

5.3.2 DeLôme Letter and Sinking of the Maine

On February 9, 1898, the newspapers published a letter written by the Spanish minister in Washington, Depuy de Lôme, personally criticizing President McKinley in insulting terms. On February 15, the Battleship U.S.S. *Maine* was blown up in Havana harbor with a loss of 250 Americans. The popular demand for war with Spain grew significantly even though it was likely that the *Maine* was blown up by accident when spontaneous combustion in a coal bunker caused a powder magazine to explode.

5.3.3 U.S. Military

Facing its first war since the Civil War, the U.S. Army was not prepared for a full scale effort in 1898. Although 245,000 men served in the war (with over 5,000 deaths), the Army at the outset consisted of only 28,000 troops. The volunteers who shaped up in the early stages were surprised to be issued winter uniforms to train in the tropics for war in Cuba. Cans of food stockpiled since the Civil War were reissued. After getting past these early problems, the War Department settled down to a more effective organizational procedure. Sadly, more deaths resulted from disease and food poisoning than from battlefield casualties. The U.S. Navy (26,000 men) was far better prepared for war as a result of past years of modernization.

5.3.4 Territories

After the United States had defeated Spain, it was faced with the issue of what to do with such captured territories as the Philippines, Puerto Rico, the Isle of Pines, and Guam. A major public debate ensued with critics of land acquisition forming the Anti-Imperialist League with the support of Mark

Twain, William James, William Jennings Bryan, Grover Cleveland, Charles Francis Adams, Carl Schurz, Charles W. Eliot, David Starr Jordan, Andrew Carnegie and Samuel Gompers, among others. Supporters of colonialism included Theodore Roosevelt, Mark Hanna, Alfred Thayer Mahan, Henry Cabot Lodge, Albert Beveridge, President McKinley and many others. Ironically, many individuals in both camps favored U.S. economic expansion, but had difficulty with the idea that a democracy would actually accept colonies and overseas armies of occupations.

5.3.5 Literature

Thorsten Veblen's *Theory of the Leisure Class* (1899) attached the "predatory wealth" and "conspicuous consumption" of the new rich in the gilded age. Veblen added evidence and argument to a critique begun by Jacob Riis in *How the Other Half Lives* (1890) documenting the gnawing poverty, illness, crime and despair of New York's slums. Frank Norris's *McTeague* (1899) chronicled a man's regression to brutish animal behavior in the dog-eat-dog world of unbridled and unregulated capitalist competition. His novel *The Octopus* (1901) condemned monopoly.

5.4   FOREIGN POLICY, 1897 – 1902

The summer war with Spain, and the expansion of American interests in Asia and the Caribbean were dominant factors.

5.4.1 Decision for War (1898)

Loss of markets, threats to Americans in Cuba, and the inability of both Spain and Cuba to resolve the Cuban revolution either by force or diplomacy led to McKinley's request of Congress for a declaration of war. The sinking of the *Maine* in February 1898, and the return of Vermont Senator Redfield Proctor from a fact-finding mission on March 17, 1898 revealed how poor the situation was in Cuba.

5.4.2 *McKinley's Ultimatum*

On March 27, President McKinley asked Spain to call an armistice, accept American mediation to end the war, and end the use of concentration camps in Cuba. When Spain refused to comply, McKinley requested Congress declare war. On April 21, Congress declared war on Spain with the objective of establishing Cuban independence (Teller Amendment).

5.4.3 *Cuba*

After the first U.S. forces landed in Cuba on June 22, 1898, the United States proceeded to victories at El Caney and San Juan Hill. By July 17, Admiral Sampson's North Atlantic Squadron destroyed the Spanish fleet, Santiago surrendered, and American troops quickly went on to capture Puerto Rico.

5.4.4 *The Philippines*

As early as December 1897, Commodore Perry's Asiatic Squadron was alerted to possible war with Spain. On May 1, 1898, the Spanish fleet in the Philippines was destroyed and Manila surrendered on August 13. Spain agreed to a peace conference to be held in Paris in October 1898.

5.4.5 *Treaty of Paris*

Secretary of State William Day led the American negotiating team which secured Cuban independence, the ceding of the

Philippines, Puerto Rico and Guam to the U.S., and the payment of $20 million to Spain for the Philippines. The treaty was ratified by the Senate on February 6, 1900.

5.4.6 *Philippines Insurrection*

Filipino nationalists under Emilio Aguinaldo rebelled against the United States (February 1899) when they learned the Philippines would not be given independence. The United States used 70,000 men to suppress the revolutionaries by June 1902. A special U.S. commission recommended eventual self-government for the Philippines.

5.4.7 *Hawaii and Wake Island*

During the war with Spain, the U.S. annexed Hawaii on July 7, 1898. In 1900 the U.S. claimed Wake Island, 2,000 miles west of Hawaii.

5.4.8 *China*

Fearing the break-up of China into separate spheres of influence, Secretary of State John Hay called for acceptance of the Open Door Notes by all nations trading in the China market to guarantee equal opportunity of trade (1899), and the sovereignty of the Manchu government of China (1900). With Manila as a base of operations, the United States was better able to protect its economic and political concerns in Asia. Such interests included the American China Development Co. (1898), a railway and mining concession in south China, and various oil, timber, and industrial investments in Manchuria.

5.4.9 Boxer Rebellion (1900)

Chinese nationalists ("Boxers") struck at foreign settlements in China, and at the Ch'ing dynasty Manchu government in Beijing for allowing foreign industrial nations such as Britain, Japan, Russia, France, Germany, Italy, Portugal, Belgium, The Netherlands, and the United States large concessions within Chinese borders. An international army helped to put down the rebellion, and aided the Chinese government to remain in power.

5.4.10 Platt Amendment (1901)

Although Cuba was granted its independence, the Platt Amendment provided that Cuba become a virtual protectorate of the United States. Cuba could not 1) make a treaty with a foreign state impairing its independence, or 2) contract an excessive public debt. Cuba was required to 1) allow the U.S. to preserve order on the island, and 2) lease a naval base for 99 years to the U.S. at Guantanamo Bay.

5.4.11 Hay-Pauncefote Treaty (1901)

This treaty between the U.S. and Britain abrogated an earlier agreement (1850, Clayton-Bulwer Treaty) to build jointly an isthmian canal. The United States was free to unilaterally construct, fortify and maintain a canal that would be open to all ships.

5.4.12 Insular Cases (1901 – 1903)

The Supreme Court decided that constitutional rights did not extend to territorial possessions, thus the Constitution did not follow the flag. Congress had the right to administer each island possession without constitutional restraint. Inhabitants of those possessions did not have the same rights as American citizens.

5.4.13 *The New Diplomacy*

As the beginning of the 20th century foreshadowed the "Americanization of the world," a modern professional foreign service was being put into place to promote the political and economic policies of a technologically and democratically advanced society about to bid for world power.

Pacific Front

THE
SPANISH –
AMERICAN
WAR

Caribbean Front

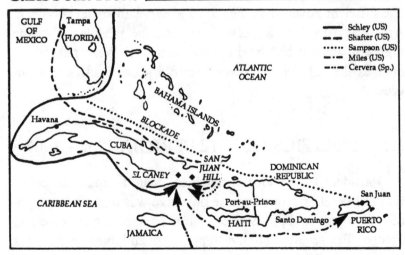

47

CHAPTER 6

THEODORE ROOSEVELT AND PROGRESSIVE REFORMS, 1902 – 1907

As a Republican progressive reformer committed to honest and efficient government designed to serve all social classes in America, Theodore Roosevelt restored the presidency to the high eminence it had held through the Civil War era, and redressed the balance of power with old guard leaders in Congress.

6.1 POLITICS OF THE PERIOD, 1902 – 1907

President Roosevelt did much to create a bipartisan coalition of liberal reformers whose objective was to restrain corporate monopoly and promote economic competition at home and abroad. Roosevelt won the support of enlightened business leaders, the middle class, consumers, and urban and rural workers with his promise of a "square deal" for all.

6.1.1 Roosevelt's Anti-Trust Policy (1902)

The president pledged strict enforcement of the Sherman Anti-Trust Act (1890) to break up illegal monopolies and regulate large corporations for the public good through honest federal government administration.

6.1.2 Progressive Reform in the States

Taking their cue from Washington, many states enacted laws creating honest and efficient political and economic regulatory standards. Political reforms included enacting laws establishing primary elections (Mississippi, Wisconsin), initiative and referendum (South Dakota, Oregon), and the rooting out of political bosses on the state and municipal levels (especially in New York, Ohio, Michigan, and California).

6.1.3 Commission Form of Government (1903)

After a hurricane and tidal wave destroyed much of Galveston, Texas, progressive businessmen and Texas state legislators removed the ineffective and corrupt mayor and city council and established a city government of five elected commissioners who were experts in their fields to rebuild Galveston. Numerous other cities adopted the commission form of government to replace the mayor/council format.

6.1.4 State Leaders

Significant state reformers in the period were Robert LaFollette of Wisconsin, Albert Cummins of Iowa, Charles Evans Hughes of New York, James M. Cox of Ohio, Hiram Johnson of California, William S. U'ren of Oregon, Albert Beveridge of Indiana, and Woodrow Wilson of New Jersey.

6.1.5 City Reformers

Urban leaders included John Purroy Mitchell of New York City, Tom L. Johnson and Newton Baker of Cleveland, Hazen Pingree of Detroit, Sam Jones of Toledo, and Joseph Folk of St. Louis.

6.1.6 Election of 1904

Having assured Republican Party leaders that he wished to reform corporate monopolies and railroads, but not interfere with monetary policy or tariffs, Roosevelt was nominated for president along with Charles Fairbanks (Indiana) for vice president. The Democratic Party nominated New York judge Alton B. Parker for president and Henry G. Davis (West Virginia) for vice president on a platform that endorsed Roosevelt's "trust-busting," which called for even greater power for such regulatory agencies as the Interstate Commerce Commission, and accepted the conservative gold standard as the basis for monetary policy. Roosevelt easily defeated Parker by about 2 million votes, and the Republicans retained control of both houses of Congress.

6.1.7 Hepburn Act (1906)

Membership of the Interstate Commerce Commission was increased from five to seven. The I.C.C. could set its own fair freight rates, had its regulatory power extended over pipelines, bridges, and express companies, and was empowered to require a uniform system of accounting by regulated transportation companies. This act and the Elkins Act (1903 – reiterated illegality of railroad rebates) gave teeth to the original Interstate Commerce Act of 1887.

6.1.8 *Pure Food and Drug Act* (1906)

Prohibited the manufacture, sale and transportation of adulterated or fraudulently labeled foods and drugs in accordance with consumer demands to which Theodore Roosevelt was especially sensitive.

6.1.9 *Meat Inspection Act* (1906)

Provided for federal and sanitary regulations and inspections in meat packing facilities. Wartime scandals in 1898 relating to spoiled canned meats were a powerful force for reform.

6.1.10 *Immunity of Witness Act* (1906)

Corporate officials could no longer make a plea of immunity to avoid testifying in cases dealing with their corporation's illegal activities.

6.1.11 *Conservation Laws*

From 1902 to 1908 a series of laws and executive actions were enacted to create federal irrigation projects, national parks and forests, develop water power (Internal Waterways Commission), and establish the National Conservation Commission to oversee the nation's resources.

6.2   THE ECONOMY, 1902 – 1907

Anti-trust policy and government regulation of the economy gave way to a more lenient enforcement of federal laws after the panic of 1907. Recognition of the rights of labor unions was enhanced.

6.2.1   *Anti-Trust Policy* (1902)

In order to restore free competition, President Roosevelt ordered the Justice Department to prosecute corporations pursuing monopolistic practices. Attorney General P.C. Knox first brought suit against the Northern Securities Co., a railroad holding corporation put together by J.P. Morgan; then he moved against Rockefeller's Standard Oil Company. By the time he left office in 1909, Roosevelt brought indictments against 25 monopolies.

6.2.2   *Department of Commerce and Labor* (1903)

A new cabinet position was created to address the concerns of business and labor. Within the department, the Bureau of Corporations was empowered to investigate and report on the illegal activities of corporations.

6.2.3   *Coal Strike* (1902)

Roosevelt interceded with government mediation to bring about negotiations between the United Mine Workers union and the anthracite mine owners after a bitter strike over wages, safety conditions and union recognition. This was the first time that the government intervened in a labor dispute without automatically siding with management.

6.2.4   *Panic of 1907*

A brief economic recession and panic occurred in 1907 as a result, in part, of questionable bank speculations, a lack of flexible monetary and credit policies, and a conservative gold standard. This event called attention to the need for banking reform which would lead to the Federal Reserve System in 1913. Although Roosevelt temporarily eased the pressure on anti-trust activity, he made it clear that reform of the economic system to promote free-enterprise capitalism would continue.

6.2.5 *St. Louis World's Fair* (1904)

The World's Fair of 1904 celebrated the centennial of the Louisiana Purchase, and brought the participation of Asian nations to promote foreign trade.

6.3 SOCIAL AND CULTURAL DEVELOPMENTS, 1902 – 1907

Debate and discussion over the expanding role of the federal government commanded the attention of the nation.

6.3.1 *Progressive Reforms*

There was not one unified progressive movement, but a series of reform causes designed to address specific social, economic and political problems. Middle class men and women were especially active in attempting to correct the excessive powers of giant corporations, and the radical extremes of Marxist revolutionaries and radicals among intellectuals and labor activists. However, the mainstreams of the business community and the labor unions were moderate in their desires to preserve economic opportunities and the free enterprise system. Progressive reforms might best be described as evolutionary change from above rather than revolutionary upheaval from below.

6.3.2 *Varieties of Reform*

Progressive reform goals included not only honest government, economic regulation, environmental conservation, labor recognition, and new political structures. Reformers also called for gender equality for men and women in the work force (Oregon Ten Hour Law), an end to racial segregation (National Association for the Advancement of Colored People), child labor laws, prison reform, regulation of the stock market, direct election of senators, and a more efficient foreign service among other reform activities.

6.3.3 *Muckrakers*

Muckrakers (a term coined by Roosevelt) were investigative journalists and authors who were often the publicity agents for reforms. Popular magazines included *McClure's, Collier's, Cosmopolitan,* and *Everybody's.* Famous articles that led to reforms included "The Shame of the Cities" by Lincoln Steffens, "History of Standard Oil Company" by Ida Tarbell, "The Treason of the Senate" by David Phillips, and "Frenzied Finance" by Thomas Lawson.

6.3.4 *Literature*

Works of literature with a social message included *Following the Color Line* by Ray Stannard Baker, *The Bitter Cry of the Children,* by John Spargo, *Poverty* by Robert Hunter, *The Story of Life Insurance* by Burton Hendrick, *The Financier* by Theodore Dreiser, *The Jungle* by Upton Sinclair, *The Boss* by Henry Lewis, *Call of the Wild, The Iron Heel* and *The War of the Classes* by Jack London, *A Certain Rich Man* by William Allen White, and *The Promise of American Life* by Herbert Croly.

6.3.5 *Inventions*

The Wright brothers made their first air flight at Kitty Hawk, North Carolina in 1903.

6.4 FOREIGN RELATIONS, 1902 – 1907

Theodore Roosevelt's "Big Stick" diplomacy and economic foreign policy were characteristics of the administration.

6.4.1 *Panama Canal*

Roosevelt used executive power to engineer the separation of Panama from Colombia, and the recognition of Panama as an independent country. The Hay-Bunau-Varilla Treaty of 1903 granted the United States control of the canal zone in Panama for $10 million and an annual fee of $250,000 beginning nine years after ratification of the treaty by both parties. Construction of the canal began in 1904 and was completed in 1914.

6.4.2 *Roosevelt Corollary to the Monroe Doctrine*

The U.S. reserved the right to intervene in the internal affairs of Latin American nations to keep European powers from using military force to collect debts in the western hemisphere. The U.S. eventually intervened in the affairs of Venezuela, Haiti, the Dominican Republic, Nicaragua, and Cuba by 1905 as an international policeman brandishing the "big stick" against Europeans and Latin Americans. Luis Drago of Argentina urged the adoption of an international agreement prohibiting the use of military force for the collection of debts.

6.4.3 Rio de Janeiro Conference (1906)

Secretary of State Elihu Root attempted to de-emphasize U.S. military and political intervention in order to promote economic and political goodwill, economic development, trade and finances in Latin America. President Roosevelt was actually moving away from "big stick" diplomacy and toward "dollar diplomacy" before he left office. The United States also promoted the Pan American Railway project at this meeting of the International Bureau of American Republics.

6.4.4 China

In pursuit of the Open Door policy of equal opportunity of trade and the guaranteed independence of China, the United States continued to promote its trade interests in Asia. Segregation and restrictions of Chinese immigrants in California and other states led Chinese national leaders to call for a boycott in 1905 of U.S. goods and services in both China and the United States. The boycott ended in 1906 without significant changes in state laws.

6.4.5 Russo-Japanese War (1904 – 1905)

With American encouragement and financial loans, Japan pursued and won a war against tsarist Russia. Roosevelt negotiated the Treaty of Portsmouth, New Hampshire, which ended the war, and for which the President ironically received the Nobel Peace Prize in 1906. Japan, however, was disappointed at not receiving more territory and financial compensation from Russia and blamed the United States.

UNITED STATES INTERESTS
IN THE FAR EAST

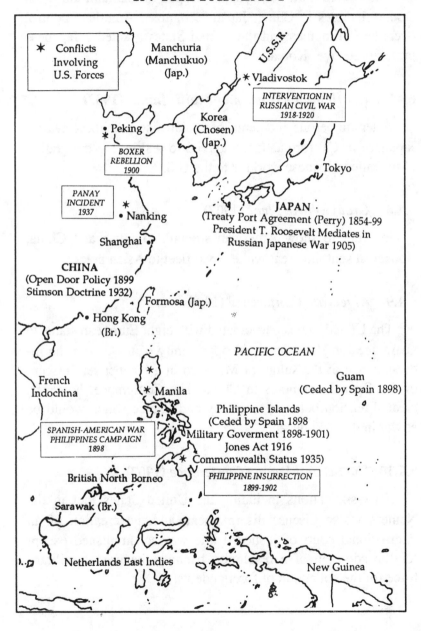

*	Conflicts Involving U.S. Forces

Manchuria (Manchukuo) (Jap.)

U.S.S.R.

* Vladivostok

INTERVENTION IN RUSSIAN CIVIL WAR 1918-1920

• Peking
*

Korea (Chosen) (Jap.)

BOXER REBELLION 1900

• Tokyo

PANAY INCIDENT 1937

*
• Nanking

JAPAN
(Treaty Port Agreement (Perry) 1854-99
President T. Roosevelt Mediates in
Russian Japanese War 1905)

Shanghai •*

CHINA
(Open Door Policy 1899
Stimson Doctrine 1932)

• Formosa (Jap.)

• Hong Kong
(Br.)

PACIFIC OCEAN

French
Indochina

*

* Manila

Guam
(Ceded by Spain 1898)

Philippine Islands
(Ceded by Spain 1898
Military Goverment 1898-1901)
Jones Act 1916

SPANISH-AMERICAN WAR
PHILIPPINES CAMPAIGN
1898

* Commonwealth Status 1935)

British North Borneo

PHILIPPINE INSURRECTION
1899-1902

Sarawak (Br.)

Netherlands East Indies

New Guinea

6.4.6   Taft-Katsura Memo (1905)

The United States and Japan pledged to maintain the Open Door principles in China. Japan recognized American control over the Philippines and the United States granted a Japanese protectorate over Korea.

6.4.7   Gentleman's Agreement with Japan (1907)

After numerous incidents of racial discrimination against Japanese in California, Japan agreed to restrict the emigration of unskilled Japanese workers to the U.S.

6.4.8   Great White Fleet (1907)

In order to show American strength to Japan and China, Roosevelt sent the great white naval fleet to Asian ports.

6.4.9   Algeciras Conference (1906)

The United States participated with eight European states to guarantee for Morocco equal opportunity of trade, and the independence of the sultan of Morocco in a manner reminiscent of the Open Door notes in China. The Conference, however, created tension between Germany and France which would be at war in the next decade.

6.4.10   The Second Hague Conference (1907)

Forty-six nations including the United States met in the Netherlands to discuss disarmament, and the creation of an international court of justice. Little was accomplished except for the adoption of a resolution banning the use of military force for the collection of foreign debts.

CHAPTER 7

THE REGULATORY STATE AND THE ORDERED SOCIETY, 1907 – 1912

The progressive presidencies of Roosevelt, Taft and Wilson brought the concept of big government to fruition. A complex corporate society needed rules and regulations as well as powerful agencies to enforce those measures necessary to maintain and enhance democratic free enterprise competition. The search for political, social and economic standards designed to preserve order in American society while still guaranteeing political, social and economic freedom was a difficult, but primary task. The nation increasingly looked to Washington to protect the less powerful segments of the republic from the special interests that had grown up in the late 19th century. A persistent problem for the federal government was how best to preserve order and standards in a complex technological society while not interfering with the basic liberties Americans came to cherish in the Constitution and throughout their history. The strain of World War I after 1914 would further complicate the problem.

7.1 POLITICS OF THE PERIOD, 1907 – 1912

The continuation of progressive reforms by both Republican and Democratic leaders helped to form a consensus for the establishment of regulatory standards.

7.1.1 *Election of 1908*

Deciding not to run for re-election, Theodore Roosevelt opened the way for William H. Taft (Ohio) and James S. Sherman (New York) to run on a Republican platform calling for a continuation of anti-trust enforcement, environmental conservation, and a lower tariff policy to promote international trade. The Democrats nominated William Jennings Bryan for a third time with John Kern (Indiana) for vice president on an anti-monopoly and low tariff platform. The Socialists once again nominated Eugene Debs. Taft easily won by over a million votes, and the Republicans retained control of both houses of Congress. For the first time, the American Federation of Labor entered national politics officially with an endorsement of Bryan. This decision began a long alliance between organized labor and the Democratic Party in the 20th century.

7.1.2 *Taft's Objectives*

The President had two primary political goals in 1909. One was the continuation of Roosevelt's trust-busting policies, and the other was the reconciliation of the old guard conservatives and young progressive reformers in the Republican Party.

7.1.3 *Anti-Trust Policy*

In pursuing anti-monopoly law enforcement, Taft chose as

his Attorney General George Wickersham, who brought 44 indictments in anti-trust suits.

7.1.4 Political Rift

Taft was less successful in healing the Republican split between conservatives and progressives over such issues as tariff reform, conservation, and the almost dictatorial power held by the reactionary Republican Speaker of the House, Joseph Cannon (Illinois). Taft's inability to bring both wings of the party together led to the hardened division which would bring about a complete Democratic victory in the 1912 elections.

7.1.5 The Anti-Cannon Crusade

In 1910, Republican progressives joined with Democrats to strip Speaker Cannon of his power to appoint the Committee on Rules and serve on it himself. Although critical of Cannon, Taft failed to align himself with the progressives. Democrats gained control of the House in the 1910 elections, and a Republican-Democratic coalition ran the Senate.

7.1.6 Ballinger-Pinchot Dispute (1909 – 1910)

Progressives backed Gifford Pinchot, chief of the U.S. Forest Service, in his charge that the conservative Secretary of the Interior, Richard Ballinger, was giving away the nation's natural resources to private corporate interests. A congressional investigatory committee found that Ballinger had done nothing illegal, but did act in a manner contrary to the government's environmental policies. Taft had supported Ballinger through the controversy, but negative public opinion forced Ballinger to resign in 1911. Taft's political standing with progressive Republicans was hurt going into the election of 1912.

7.1.7 Government Efficiency

Taft promoted the idea of a national budgetary system. Although Congress refused to cooperate, by executive action the President saved over $40 million for the government, and set an example for many state and local governments.

7.1.8 The Sixteenth Amendment

Congress passed in 1909 a graduated income tax amendment to the Constitution which was ratified in 1913.

7.1.9 Mann-Elins Act (1910)

This act extended the regulatory function of the Interstate Commerce Commission over cable and wireless companies, and telephone and telegraph lines; gave the I.C.C. power to begin its own court proceedings and suspend questionable rates; and set up a separate but temporary commerce court to handle rate dispute cases.

7.1.10 Election of 1912

This election was one of the most dramatic in American history. President Taft's inability to maintain party harmony led Theodore Roosevelt to return to national politics. When denied the Republican nomination, Roosevelt and his supporters formed the Progressive Party (Bull Moose) and nominated Roosevelt for president and Hiram Johnson (California) for vice president on a political platform nicknamed "The New Nationalism". It called for stricter regulation on large corporations, creation of a tariff commission, women's suffrage, minimum wages and benefits, direct election of senators, initiative, referendum and recall, presidential primaries, and prohibition of child labor. Roosevelt also called for a Federal Trade Commission to regulate the broader economy, a stronger executive, and more government planning. Theodore Roosevelt did not see big business as evil, but a permanent development that was necessary in a modern economy.

7.1.11 The Republicans

President Taft and Vice President Sherman retained control of the Republican Party after challenges by Roosevelt and Robert LaFollette, and were nominated on a platform of "Quiet Confidence" calling for a continuation of progressive programs pursued by Taft over the past four years.

7.1.12 The Democrats

After forty-five ballots without a nomination, the Democratic convention finally worked out a compromise whereby William Jennings Bryan gave his support to New Jersey Governor Woodrow Wilson on the forty-sixth ballot. Thomas Marshall (Indiana) was chosen as the vice presidential candidate. Wilson called his campaign the "New Freedom" based on progressive programs similar to those in the Progressive and Republican parties. Wilson, however, did not agree with Roosevelt on the issue of big business, which Wilson saw as morally evil. Therefore Wilson called for breaking up large corporations rather than just regulating them. He differed from the other two party candidates by favoring independence for the Philippines, and the exemption from prosecution of labor unions under the Sherman Anti-Trust Act. Wilson also supported such measures as lower tariffs, a graduated income tax, banking reform, and direct election of senators. Philosophically, Wilson was skeptical of big business and big government. In some respects, he hoped to return to an earlier and simpler concept of a free enterprise republic. After his selection, however, he would modify his views to conform more with those of Theodore Roosevelt.

7.1.13 Election Results

The Republican split clearly paved the way for Wilson's victory. Wilson received 6.2 million votes, Roosevelt 4.1 million, Taft 3.5 million, and the Socialist Debs 900,000 votes. In the electoral college, Wilson received 435 votes, Roosevelt 88, Taft 8. Although a minority president, Wilson garnered the largest electoral majority in American history to that time. Democrats won control of both houses of Congress.

7.1.14 *The Wilson Presidency*

The Wilson administration brought together many of the policies and initiatives of the previous Republican administrations, and reform efforts in Congress by both parties. Before the outbreak of World War I in 1914, President Wilson, working with cooperative majorities in both houses of Congress, achieved much of the remaining progressive agenda including lower tariff reform (Underwood-Simmons Act, 1913), the 16th Amendment (graduated income tax, 1913), the 17th Amendment (direct election of Senators, 1913), Federal Reserve Banking System (which provided regulation and flexibility to monetary policy, 1913), Federal Trade Commission (to investigate unfair business practices, 1914), and the Clayton Anti-Trust Act (improving the old Sherman Act and protecting labor unions and farm cooperatives from prosecution, 1914).

Other goals such as the protection of children in the work force (Keating-Owen Act, 1916), credit reform for agriculture

(Federal Farm Loan Act, 1916), and an independent tariff commission (1916) came later. By the end of Wilson's presidency, the New Freedom and the New Nationalism merged into one government philosophy of regulation, order and standardization in the interest of an increasingly diverse and pluralistic American nation.

7.2 THE ECONOMY, 1907 – 1912

The short-lived panic of 1907 revealed economic weaknesses in banking and currency policy addressed by Presidents Roosevelt, Taft and Wilson, and by Congress. Significantly, the American economy was strengthened just in time to meet the challenges of World War I.

7.2.1 *National Monetary Commission* (1908)

Chaired by Senator Nelson Aldrich (Rhode Island), the 18 member commission recommended what later became the basis for the Federal Reserve System in 1913 with a secure Treasury reserve and branch banks to add and subtract currency from the monetary supply depending on the needs of the economy.

7.2.2 *Payne-Aldrich Tariff* (1909)

Despite the intention of lowering the tariff, enough amendments were added in the Senate to turn the bill into a protective measure. Progressive reformers felt betrayed by special interests opposed to consumer price concerns. President Taft made the political mistake of endorsing the tariff.

7.2.3 *Postal Savings Banks* (1910)

Recommended by President Taft, and one of the original

Populist Party goals, certain U.S. post offices were authorized to receive deposits and pay interest.

7.2.4 New Battleship Contract, 1910

The State Department arranged for Bethlehem Steel Corporation to receive a large contract to build battleships for Argentina. This was an example of Taft's "dollar diplomacy" in action.

7.2.5 Anti-Trust Proceedings

Although a friend to the business community, President Taft ordered 90 legal proceedings against monopolies, and 44 anti-trust suits including the one which broke up the American Tobacco Trust (1911). It was also under Taft that the government succeeded with its earlier suit against Standard Oil.

7.2.6 Canadian Reciprocity, 1911

A reciprocal trade agreement between the United States and Canada was repudiated by the Canadian legislature, which feared economic and political domination by the United States.

7.2.7 New Cabinet Posts, 1913

The Department of Commerce and Labor was divided into two separate autonomous cabinet level positions.

7.2.8 Automobiles

In 1913 Henry Ford introduced the continuous flow process on the automobile assembly line.

7.3 SOCIAL AND CULTURAL DEVELOPMENTS, 1907 – 1912

The rationale for progressive reform and government activism were important themes in American society (see Chapter 6).

7.3.1 Social Programs

States led the way with programs such as public aid to mothers of dependent children (Illinois, 1911), and the first minimum wage law (Massachusetts, 1912).

7.3.2 Race and Ethnic Attitudes

Despite the creation of the NAACP in 1909, many progressive reformers tended to be Anglo-Saxon elitists critical of the lack of accomplishments of Native American Indians, African-Americans, and Asian, Southern and Eastern European immigrants. In 1905, the African-American intellectual militant W.E.B. DuBois founded the Niagara Movement calling for federal legislation to protect racial equality, and full rights of citizenship.

7.3.3 Radical Labor

Although moderate labor unions as represented by the A.F. of L. functioned within the American system, a radical labor organization called the Industrial Workers of the World (I.W.W. or Wobblies, 1905 – 1924) was active in promoting violence and revolution. Led by colorful figures such as Carlo Tresca, Elizabeth Gurley Flynn (the Red Flame), Daniel DeLeon, "Mother" Mary Harris Jones, the maverick priest Father Thomas Hagerty, and Big Bill Haywood, among others, the I.W.W. organized effective strikes in the textile industry in 1912, and among a few western miners groups, but generally had little appeal to the average American worker. After the Red Scare of 1919, the government worked to smash the I.W.W. and deport many of its immigrant leaders and members.

7.3.4 White Slave Trade

In 1910, Congress made interstate prostitution a federal crime with passage of the Mann Act.

7.3.5 Literature

Enthused by the self-confidence exuded by political reformers, writers remained optimistic in their realism, and their faith in the American people to solve social and economic problems with honest and efficient programs (see Chapter 6).

7.3.6 Motion Pictures

By 1912 Hollywood had replaced New York and New Jersey as the center for silent film production. There were 13,000 movie houses in the United States and Paramount Pictures had just been formed as a large studio resembling other large corporations. Serials, epic features and Mack Sennett comedies were in production. All of these developments contributed to the "star system" in American film entertainment.

7.3.7 Science

The X-ray tube was developed by William Coolidge in 1913. Robert Goddard patented liquid rocket fuel in 1914. Plastics and synthetic fibers such as rayon were developed in

1909 by Arthur Little and Leo Baekeland respectively. Adolphus Busch applied the Diesel engine to the submarine in 1912.

7.4   FOREIGN RELATIONS, 1907 – 1912

The expansion of American international interests through Taft's "dollar diplomacy," and world tensions foreshadowing the First World War were dominant themes.

7.4.1   *Dollar Diplomacy*

President Taft sought to avoid military intervention, especially in Latin America, by replacing "big stick" policies with "dollar diplomacy" in the expectation that American financial investments would encourage economic, social and political stability. This idea proved an illusion as investments never really filtered through all levels of Latin American societies, nor did such investments generate democratic reforms.

7.4.2   *Mexican Revolution* (1910)

Francisco I. Madero overthrew the dictator Porfirio Diaz (1911) declaring himself a progressive revolutionary akin to reformers in the United States. American and European corporate interests (especially oil and mining) feared national interference with their investments in Mexico. President Taft recognized Madero's government, but stationed 10,000 troops on the Texas border (1912) to protect Americans from the continuing fighting. In 1913 Madero was assassinated by General Victoriano Huerta. Wilson urged Huerta to hold democratic elections and adopt a constitutional government. When Huerta refused his advice, Wilson invaded Mexico with troops at Vera Cruz in 1914. A second U.S. invasion came in northern Mexico in 1916. War between the U.S. and Mexico might have occurred had not World War I intervened.

7.4.3 *Pan American Mediation* (1914)

John Barrett, head of the Pan American Union (formerly Blaine's International Bureau of American Republics) called for multilateral mediation to bring about a solution to Mexico's internal problems, and extract the United States from its military presence in Mexico. Although Wilson initially refused, Argentina, Brazil and Chile did mediate among the Mexican factions and Wilson withdrew American troops. Barrett hoped to replace the unilateral Monroe Doctrine with a multilateral Pan American policy to promote collective responses and mediation to difficult hemispheric problems. Wilson, however, refused to share power with Latin America.

7.4.4 *Latin American Interventions*

Although Taft and Secretary of State P.C. Knox created the Latin American Division of the State Department in 1909 to promote better relations, the United States kept a military presence in the Dominican Republic and Haiti, and intervened militarily in Nicaragua (1911) to quiet fears of revolution and help manage foreign financial problems

7.4.5 *Arbitration Treaties*

Taking a page from Roosevelt's book, Taft promoted arbitration agreements as an alternative to war in Latin America and in Asia.

7.4.6 *Lodge Corollary to the Monroe Doctrine* (1911)

When a Japanese syndicate moved to purchase a large tract

of land in Mexico's Lower California, Senator Lodge introduced a resolution to block the Japanese investment. The Corollary went further to exclude non-European powers from the western hemisphere under the Monroe Doctrine.

7.4.7 Bryan's Arbitration Treaties (1913 – 1915)

Wilson's Secretary of State William Jennings Bryan continued the policies of Roosevelt and Taft to promote arbitration of disputes in Latin America and elsewhere. Bryan negotiated about 30 such treaties.

7.4.8 Root-Takahira Agreement (1908)

This agreement reiterated the status quo in Asia established by the United States and Japan by the Taft-Katsura Memo (1905) (see Chapter 6).

7.4.9 China Consortium (1909)

American bankers and the State Department demanded entry into an international banking association with Britain, France and Germany to build a railway network (Hukuang) in southern and central China. Wilson withdrew the U.S. from participation in 1913 as the Chinese revolution deteriorated into greater instability.

7.4.10 Manchuria

President Taft and Secretary Knox attempted to force the sale of Japanese and Russian railroad interests in Manchuria to American investment interests. When this diplomacy failed, Knox moved to construct a competing rail system. The Chinese government, however, refused to approve the American plan.

Both Japan and Russia grew more suspicious of United States interests in Asia.

7.4.11 *Chinese Revolution, 1911*

Chinese nationalists overthrew the Manchu Dynasty and the last emperor of China, Henry Pu Yi. Although the military warlord Yuan Shih-Kai seized control, decades of factionalism, revolution and civil war destabilized China and its market potential for American and other foreign investors.

7.4.12 *World War I, 1914 – 1919*

European strife in the years 1907 to 1912 were warnings of the conflict to come. By this time, the competing military alliance system of Germany, Austria-Hungary and Turkey (Triple Alliance or Central Powers), and France, Russia and Britain (Triple Entente) was already in place, and a major arms race had been underway for some time. Conflicts between Germany and France over Morocco occurred in 1905, 1908, and 1911, and brought the two powers to the brink of war. In 1908, the Bosnian Crisis in the Balkans brought Austria-Hungary into conflict with Tsarist Russia. In 1912 Balkan wars occurred when Russia urged Serbia, Bulgaria, Greece and Montenegro to go to war with Turkey. With a victory over Turkey, the Balkan states began fighting among themselves. Austria was suspicious of Pan Slavism encouraged by Russia in the Balkans. When the heir to the Austrian Hapsburg Empire was assassinated in 1914, Austria moved to crush Pan Slavism in Serbia. Russian intervention led in turn to German, French, British and Turkish participation. World War I had begun. The United States attempted to maintain a neutrality of sorts but was drawn into the conflict in 1917.

7.4.13 Consequences of War

The impact of the war was far-reaching in the 20th century. The United States emerged as the economic and political leader of the world – even if the American people were not prepared to accept the responsibility. The Russian revolution overthrew the tsar and inaugurated a communist dictatorship. Britain, France, Austria, and Turkey went into various states of decline. Germany was devastated at the Versailles Peace Conference. Revenge and bitterness would contribute to the rise of Adolph Hitler and the Nazi movement. The European industrial nations would never recover from the cost of the war. Lingering economic problems would contribute to the Crash of 1929 and the Great Depression of the 1930s. The seeds of World War II had been planted.

"The ESSENTIALS" of
ACCOUNTING & BUSINESS

Each book in the **Accounting and Business ESSENTIALS** series offers all essential information about the subject it covers. It includes every important principle and concept, and is designed to help students in preparing for exams and doing homework. The **Accounting and Business ESSENTIALS** are excellent supplements to any class text or course of study.

The **Accounting and Business ESSENTIALS** are complete and concise, with quick access to needed information. They also provide a handy reference source at all times. The **Accounting and Business ESSENTIALS** are prepared with REA's customary concern for high professional quality and student needs.

Available titles include:

Accounting I & II	**Cost & Managerial Accounting I &**
Advanced Accounting I & II	**Financial Management**
Advertising	**Income Taxation**
Auditing	**Intermediate Accounting I & II**
Business Law I & II	**Macroeconomics I & II**
Business Statistics I & II	**Marketing Principles**
College & University Writing	**Microeconomics**
Corporate Taxation	**Money & Banking I & II**

If you would like more information about any of these books,
complete the coupon below and return it to us or go to your local bookstore.

RESEARCH & EDUCATION ASSOCIATION
61 Ethel Road W. • Piscataway, New Jersey 08854
Phone: (732) 819-8880

Please send me more information about your Accounting & Business Essentials Books

Name _____

Address _____

City _____ State _____ Zip _____

REA's Test Preps
The Best in Test Preparation

- REA "Test Preps" are **far more** comprehensive than any other test preparation series
- Each book contains up to **eight** full-length practice exams based on the most recent exams
- **Every** type of question likely to be given on the exams is included
- Answers are accompanied by **full** and **detailed** explanations

REA has published over 60 Test Preparation volumes in several series. They include:

Advanced Placement Exams (APs)
Biology
Calculus AB & Calculus BC
Chemistry
Computer Science
English Language & Composition
English Literature & Composition
European History
Government & Politics
Physics
Psychology
Spanish Language
Statistics
United States History

**College-Level Examination
  Program (CLEP)**
American History I
Analysis & Interpretation of
  Literature
College Algebra
Freshman College Composition
General Examinations
General Examinations Review
Human Growth and Development
Introductory Sociology
Principles of Marketing
Spanish

SAT II: Subject Tests
American History
Biology
Chemistry
English Language Proficiency Test
French

SAT II: Subject Tests (continued)
German
Literature
Mathematics Level IC, IIC
Physics
Spanish
Writing

Graduate Record Exams (GREs)
Biology
Chemistry
Computer Science
Economics
Engineering
General
History
Literature in English
Mathematics
Physics
Political Science
Psychology
Sociology

ACT - American College Testing
  Assessment

ASVAB - Armed Services Vocational
  Aptitude Battery

CBEST - California Basic Educational
  Skills Test

CDL - Commercial Driver's License Exam

CLAST - College Level Academic Skills
  Test

ELM - Entry Level Mathematics

ExCET - Exam for Certification of
  Educators in Texas

FE (EIT) - Fundamentals of
  Engineering Exam

FE Review - Fundamentals of
  Engineering Review

GED - High School Equivalency
  Diploma Exam (US & Canadian
  editions)

GMAT - Graduate Management
  Admission Test

LSAT - Law School Admission Test

MAT - Miller Analogies Test

MCAT - Medical College Admission
  Test

MSAT - Multiple Subjects
  Assessment for Teachers

NJ HSPT- New Jersey High School
  Proficiency Test

PPST - Pre-Professional Skills Tests

PRAXIS II/NTE - Core Battery

PSAT - Preliminary Scholastic
  Assessment Test

SAT I - Reasoning Test

SAT I - Quick Study & Review

TASP - Texas Academic Skills
  Program

TOEFL - Test of English as a
  Foreign Language

RESEARCH & EDUCATION ASSOCIATION
61 Ethel Road W. • Piscataway, New Jersey 08854
Phone: (732) 819-8880

Please send me more information about your Test Prep Books

Name _____

Address _____

City _____ State _____ Zip _____

"The ESSENTIALS" of HISTORY

REA's **Essentials of History** series offers a new approach to the study of history that is differe from what has been available previously. Compared with conventional history outlines, the **Essentia of History** offer far more detail, with fuller explanations and interpretations of historical events a developments. Compared with voluminous historical tomes and textbooks, the **Essentials of Histo** offer a far more concise, less ponderous overview of each of the periods they cover.

The **Essentials of History** provide quick access to needed information, and will serve as a han reference source at all times. The **Essentials of History** are prepared with REA's customary conce for high professional quality and student needs.

UNITED STATES HISTORY
1500 to 1789 From Colony to Republic
1789 to 1841 The Developing Nation
1841 to 1877 Westward Expansion & the Civil War
1877 to 1912 Industrialism, Foreign Expansion & the Progressive Era
1912 to 1941 World War I, the Depression & the New Deal
America since 1941: Emergence as a World Power

WORLD HISTORY
Ancient History (4,500 BC to AD 500)
The Emergence of Western Civilization
Medieval History (AD 500 to 1450)
The Middle Ages

EUROPEAN HISTORY
1450 to 1648 The Renaissance, Reformatior & Wars of Religion
1648 to 1789 Bourbon, Baroque & the Enlightenment
1789 to 1848 Revolution & the New European Order
1848 to 1914 Realism & Materialism
1914 to 1935 World War I & Europe in Cris
Europe since 1935: From World War II to th Demise of Communism

CANADIAN HISTORY
Pre-Colonization to 1867
The Beginning of a Nation
1867 to Present
The Post-Confederate Nation

*If you would like more information about any of these books,
complete the coupon below and return it to us or go to your local bookstore.*

RESEARCH & EDUCATION ASSOCIATION
61 Ethel Road W. • Piscataway, New Jersey 08854
Phone: (732) 819-8880

Please send me more information about your History Essentials Books

Name _____

Address _____

City _____ State _____ Zip _____